Ready
Aim
Fire!

A Practical Guide to Setting and Achieving Goals

By
Erik Fisher and Jim Woods

Disclaimer

The information in this book is based on the opinions, knowledge, and experience of the authors. All quotes are used with permission or are cited in the notes section. The authors will not be held liable for the use or misuse of the information contained herein.

"Give me a stock clerk with a goal, and I'll give you a man who will make history. Give me a man with no goals, and I'll give you a stock clerk."   J. C. Penney

Table of Contents

Preface

As the host of the Beyond The To-Do List Podcast, I spend a lot of time talking about productivity. Over the years, I've come to a conclusion: productivity is really about learning how to become more awesome.

We all learn in different ways. What works for me, may not work for you, and that's fine. But there are some common threads that connect in "being awesome." One of the most important things you can do is have goals based on your priorities, and use baby steps to accomplish them. Your plan also needs to focus on what matters to you or you will give up.

Use this tool and mesh it with your personality. Let it make you stronger, and more awesome. Be like Tony Stark—he is the same person with or without his Iron Man suit.

Erik Fisher

It all started with a phone call. Erik told me he was coming into Nashville and I called to see when we could meet for coffee. We chatted a briefly and I told him I had been writing a book about productivity.

Erik replied enthusiastically that he was working on a productivity book as well and we planned on meeting the next morning after a speech he was giving.

As soon as I heard Erik's keynote, I was certain I would work with him. His approach was down to earth, realistic, and most importantly family-focused.

After the presentation, what I assumed would be a twenty minute chat turned into an hour and a half in depth conversation. What would it take to transform lives—to really have lasting change?

It became clear it would take more than one book on productivity. So on that note, you hold in your hands the first book of three. This is the first step in a thousand mile journey.

Jim Woods

Introduction

We all have the same amount of time in the week—168 hours. But some people—you know, those really successful people who accomplish so many tasks that you think they are superhuman—seem get so much more done.

How do they do it? Are they incredibly focused, disciplined robots?

What's the secret? Can you too be really successful? Can you be disciplined and still have freedom?

Yes, you can—without a doubt! Remove impossible from your vocabulary. It's time to accomplish goals you have only dreamed about. It's time to get healthier, start your business, write your book, or learn a new language.

Whatever you've been putting off, the time is now! Whether you are disorganized, frustrated, or overwhelmed, let's leave regrets in the past and instead take things one step at a time. Most goals can be achieved in 30 days. Start now, and you are that much closer to success.

In school you learned how to read, write, and do math, but you probably weren't taught how to set and achieve goals.

This book is a step-by-step process to help you set goals in order to pursue what matters most to you.

Whether you want to start a business, write a book, or spend more time with your family, this book is for you. Each page gives you information, inspiration, and an action step to apply to fit the goal you choose to set.

This book is first in a series of three. This volume is dedicated to helping you focus on priorities and achieve goals. You can read this book in three different ways: all in one sitting, as a daily reading one entry per day, or both. The advantage to doing both is that you can first have an overview and then dive into the details as you work through the process of achieving your goal.

No matter which option you choose, you are encouraged to read this with a notepad in hand—participate in the action steps, and you will experience intentional growth.

Ready, Aim, Fire!

All projects, goals, and endeavors have step-by-step processes. Think about a target. To hit the target, you don't just randomly fire at it. Instead, you follow a step-by-step process—ready, aim, fire!

When you take intentional steps, one step builds on the other. This book starts at the very beginning and walks you through the process of choosing a goal and then taking you step by step through the process to achieve it.

The majority of projects can be simplified into three steps: the beginning, the middle, and the end. This concept can easily be applied to goals too: Ready is the beginning; Aim is the middle; and Fire is the end. This book will help you with all three stages, but you must do the work.

All three steps are important, and no step is more important than the other. It's when you follow the logical order that you have the most success. Let's look closer at each stage.

Ready. This stage is filled with preparation. It could mean doing your homework, taking time to rest, or spending hours in practice. A portion of the time will be spent waiting. Research is likely involved.

This step is not a glamorous. It means learning—which looks different for each of us. It is easy to get lost in this process because of lack of intentionality. A million rabbit holes and tangents await. Research—especially with the internet and tabbed browsing in particular—requires intentionality.

Getting ready requires work, so it's easy to mistake this step with the "Fire" stage. For a writer, it could mean writing on a blog as a way of preparing for a book. For a musician, it may mean learning new songs or recording them. Don't assume that this stage is an easy stage or shrug this off as not important. When you want to do something, you need to be prepared. You will face challenges ahead and have to prepare for them. The "Ready" stage is often time spent removing excuses and facing resistance. Why else do you want to clean the apartment or do your taxes when you should be writing your novel or business plan?

Aim. This time is one of focusing and setting the scope. Zooming in. Committing. Saying no to other things. Looking at one target, not several. If you want to be successful, understand that the efficiency of multitasking is a myth. Sure, you can get more done—but in a mediocre way. Multitasking is the enemy of excellence. You do not have an endless supply of energy or focus. Both are finite resources. You can do only one thing at a time. It's that simple ... and that difficult.

Fire. This stage is a time of executing. It's "go time." Putting in the work, not finding new targets. Action. You yourself have to do this; no one else can do this for you. It means closing the door and grinding through the work. Staying up late and getting up early. This step is what separates the professionals from the amateurs. Some like to talk about doing things; others like to actually do them. Execute—which means putting in the work—and you will quickly separate yourself from the rest.

This step-by-step process will look different for each of us, and that's fine. It's time to start accomplishing your goals!

Why Set Goals in the First Place?

Goals are essential to your success.

> *"A winner is someone who recognizes his God-given talents, works his tail off to develop them into skills, and uses these skills to accomplish his goals." Larry Bird*

Goals give focus and direction.

Goals require intentionality. A ship doesn't just leave the harbor and find the destination by chance. The captain has already chosen a port and has charted a course. When you have a goal in place, you know which direction to go.

Goals encourage growth. You should set goals that make you stretch in order to reach them.

Goals provide measurement. When you pursue a goal, you document the situation. If you fail, you can analyze the situation, learn from it, and move forward. If you succeed, you can look back and figure out how you achieved your goal.

To achieve your goals, it is essential to write them down. A study by Dominican University revealed that those who had written goals dramatically increased their success rate from 43% to 61% in contrast to those who did not write down their goals. If you write down your goals, create action plans for them, and have weekly accountability, the success rate goes up to 76%.[2]

This book will take you step by step through the process from the development of a goal that matters to you to the fulfillment of it.

Make no mistake about it—success is found when you combine hard work, time, and intentional goals.

> *"Everyone wants to improve their life. We can have these big ambitions, but if we don't break those down and set specific goals, we're not ever going to get anywhere."* Crystal Paine

You are at the beginning of the path. Just buying this book shows you are serious about intentional growth. It's time to take some of your first steps. Ready? Good. Let's go.

Where Are You Now?

Where are you right now in life? This is the first question to answer before anything else. If you know where you are now, you have an idea which way to go in the future.

Each day is an opportunity to grow and to move in the direction you choose.

Whether you are in college or married with kids, your life constantly changes. A college student with the first class at 11:00 a.m. can easily stay up until 3:00 a.m. Parents of a newborn reshape their sleep schedules around the needs of the child.

Each season of life requires different things. No one else will have the same schedule, needs, or goals as you. So with this in mind, customize what you would like to do to fit your current schedule. It may not be possible to accomplish all you want to do in this season of your life—and that's all right.

"It may not be the best time for you. Once you determine this is the right time, make sure you aren't sacrificing something that is more important for something that is less important. Then you can talk about where a platform fits in.

"Maybe it fits in at night like it did for me after the kids are in bed, or on Saturday morning for a couple of hours before everybody's really up. It's a matter of scheduling it so you don't throw your life out of balance by focusing on one thing to the exclusion of everything else." Michael Hyatt

Do what you can right now.

Action Step: Take five minutes to write down what you are doing so that you can evaluate what season you are in right now. Be realistic.

Dad—Infant son is teething, and toddler has a lot of energy.
Husband—Needs to help wife even more with kids.
Employee—Busiest season at work until fall, so a few more hours are required.
Writer—Write one blog post per week.

What season are you in right now? What are some of the roles you are playing? Answer this in the space provided.

What Are Your Priorities?

Your priorities should be what drive you to where you want to go.

> *"The life you have left is a gift. Cherish it. Enjoy it now, to the fullest. Do what matters, now."* Leo Babauta

Often there is a disconnect between what you think your priorities are and what you spend your time doing. You can name God and family as priorities, but if you spend all of your time watching TV, what are your real priorities?

> *"Action expresses priorities."* Gandhi

How you spend your time shows what your priorities are.

Intentionally pursue what matters to you.

Action Step: Write down your priorities. What do you spend most of your time on? How does this match up with your priorities?

God
Spouse
Kids
Money
Health
Career
Hobbies
Fun

What are your priorities?

What do you spend your time doing? Are you intentional with your time?

Get More Perspective

When you examine your priorities, you see them from your own perspective. Your emotions, stress, or even lack of sleep can mislead you. If you are filled with fear or doubt, it is hard to make rational decisions because your perspective is skewed.

> *"We need a variety of input and influence and voices. You cannot get all the answers to life and business from one person or from one source."*
> *Jim Rohn*

An outside perspective is needed to look objectively at the situation. Find someone who will be completely honest but has your best interests at heart. With this additional perspective, you can set a better goal.

You cannot see your own blind spots, but others can reveal them to you.

Action Step: Ask for input about your priorities from five individuals you trust. Do not just ask family members if you want the most accurate response. Include your coworkers, friends, neighbors, and colleagues. Yes, this can be scary to do—but it is definitely worth it.

Send a short simple email or text such as this: Hi there! I need some help! Can you tell me what you see as my top three priorities? Thank you so much for your input!

Which five people do you want input from?

1.

2.

3.

4.

5.

How will you contact each person? Be specific and then make it happen!

1.

2.

3.

4.

5.

Dig Deeper on Perspective

Once you've received a response, ask yourself, "What can I do with this feedback? How can I figure out what to listen to and what to ignore?"

Look for common patterns or trends. Remember that you chose whom to ask and that you chose those individuals for a reason: you value their opinions.

If the answers seem to conflict with one another, ask for more information. Be specific. With each question you ask, you move closer to clarity and learning more about yourself.

Action Step: Analyze the responses you've received. If needed, follow up and ask additional questions. Write down your thoughts, and know that you are moving closer toward establishing your priorities. Once those are established, you can set a goal that is important to you.

Example

Priorities given from feedback: (1) kids, (2) family, (3) writing, and (4) career.

What were the responses from those you trust?

If you want one of your priorities to be a daily devotional time with God or more quality time with your spouse, but your spouse or faith was not mentioned in the responses, it is likely you have found a priority to focus on. But don't set a goal yet. Just make a note of it, and you can come back to it later.

Remember—dramatic change doesn't happen overnight. Right now you are in the "Ready" stage, doing research, so you haven't committed to anything yet.

This Is the Wheel of Your Life

In this diagram each portion represents a specific area of your life. Your life might not have seven parts to it right now, and that's completely fine. In a perfect world, your life's activities would include doing something in each of the seven areas. But let's face it: if you want to start a business, going to parties is probably not very high on your to-do list.

This exercise is important to help you determine what area to set your goal in. And what you do in one area of your life impacts the others. For example, if you aren't healthy physically, it is hard to have intellectual growth and spiritual growth when you are sick or often tired.

Action Step: Give each segment a number between 1 and 10 (1 being unsatisfied; 10 being completely satisfied). Take no more than 10 minutes to do this. Use a timer if necessary.

Example
Career: 5
Financial: 8
Spiritual: 7
Physical: 2
Intellectual: 6
Family: 3
Social: 9

What are your numbers for the wheel?

Career:
Financial:
Spiritual:
Physical:
Intellectual:
Family:
Social:

Looking Closer at the Wheel of Your Life

Refer to your "wheel of your life" diagram you drew. Congratulations! Just by completing this exercise, you have done something the majority of people never do!

Let's examine the wheel you made. Why did you give those scores? What feels most out of balance on your wheel? If this challenge feels overwhelming, feel free to focus on just one area of the wheel, or take some extra time for this exercise.

Action Step: Look at your results and dig deeper by writing out specifically what you are doing (or not doing) in each area.

Examples

Career—just received promotion but not satisfied
Financial—sticking to budget and saving more
Spiritual—ushering at church, daily devotion and   meditation, and weekly Bible study
Physical—not working out, eating junk food
Intellectual—reading a book a month
Family—quality time with kids but very little quality time with spouse
Social—parties, gatherings at church, meeting friends for dinner

Why did you assign the number you did for the Wheel of Your Life?

Career

Financial

Spiritual

Physical

Intellectual

Family

Social

Reflection: What Needs to Change?

The "wheel of your life" is a great tool to analyze your life, but keep in mind that it is impossible to change all aspects of your life at the same time.

> *"Pick the one thing that's going to make the biggest difference. Focus on the one area that feels like it's dragging all the other areas down. As you come up with all these other ideas of things that you want to change, write them down and keep a running list and once you've implemented that one thing, and it's become a habit, it just happens without you thinking about it, then add in the next one, and make that a habit. Slow and steady, instead of trying to do everything at once." Crystal Paine*

Let's narrow things down. You probably know what you want to change, but let's bring it to the forefront of your mind.

Action Step: Look at the two categories with the lowest numbers in your wheel. What would success look like for each those areas?

Examples

Physical had score of 2. Success is reaching my optimal weight, lower cholesterol, having more energy, and not feeling tired all of the time

Family had score of 3. Success is more attention on spouse; intimacy, good communication, time together on dates

In the example above, just having more energy and feeling better will very likely help increase communication and intimacy with your spouse. If you physically don't feel well, you find it much easier to veg out on the couch and watch TV than to engage in conversation.

What would success look like in your two lowest scores?

Do you see a connection between those two areas of your life?

Make a SMART Goal

It's time to write down your goal. The goals with the most clarity are SMART goals, a concept from George T. Doran.

SMART goals are easy to break into smaller tasks and to follow up on, since the goals are so specific.

Specific — Who? What? When? Where? Which?
Measurable — How much? How many?
Achievable — Is it realistic?
Relevant — Does it matter?
Timely — Is it time sensitive?

> *"A good goal is like a strenuous exercise—it makes you stretch." Mary Kay Ash*

Action Step: Look over your notes, and write out your SMART Goal. If you are not sure what goal you want to set, don't worry! Go back to the "wheel of your life" page, and look at your priorities. One specific area will jump out at you. Give it 48 hours, and then write it down in a SMART way.

If you are still stuck after 4 hours, you can't ever go wrong with focusing on your physical health, as it effects everything you do.

Examples

Lose 10 lbs. by working out on my lunch hour three times a week over the next 90 days.

Go on family vacation to Disney World in July by sticking to the household budget and saving $10,000.

What is the SMART goal you want to accomplish?

What Fuels Your Goals?

Many times if you don't achieve a goal, it is because the motivation was based solely on one thing. Life happens, and you get busy, distracted, or tired. Then it is really easy to lose focus.

> *"We all need a carrot dangling there—something to be working toward. If you don't have a specific goal, good luck finding motivation."* Bryan Allain

What if you have not one, not two, but seven reasons to work on your goal?

> *"Strong reasons make strong actions."* William Shakespeare

These reasons will support and encourage you while you pursue your goal.

Action Step: List the reasons you want to pursue your goal. Write as many as possible.

Post this list somewhere you will see often so it can remind and inspire you.

Example

Reasons I am pursuing a goal of starting a business

I am starting a business to serve God.

I am starting a business to help others.

I am starting a business to use my gifts.

I am starting a business so that I can spend more time with my family.

I am starting a business to provide for my wife and kids financially.

I am starting a business to leave a legacy that matters.

I am starting a business to have fun and grow.

Now it's your turn. Write out your reasons list on the next page.

If you are having a hard time, try applying your goal to the Wheel of your Life on Page 18.

Your goal:

Reasons you are pursuing your goal:

Use the KISS Method

Life is really complicated sometimes, isn't it?

But it doesn't always have to be that way. In the areas you can control, "KISS" your troubles away.

Keep
It
Simple,
Smartypants (or Stupid, if you prefer)

Life is complicated because we often focus on things that cannot be controlled. Aim toward one goal, and you are much more likely to succeed than if you try to hit several at the same time.

Why not treat your goals like the classic Nintendo® game Duck Hunt? The premise of the game was to shoot ducks with the gun-shaped controller. You fired at the two ducks released, not the ducks that had flown away. You focused on one target, shot at it, and then moved to the next one and shot it. If you aimed at two targets at once, you missed both almost every time.

Just work on the task at hand; don't worry about other things you want to do later. Don't worry about another project you need to do a month from now or an upcoming task you have not done before. You will get to those later.

Simplify your current tasks, and continually narrow them down as you move forward. Do not widen the scope of your project, no matter what. Those great ideas that pop up when working on your goal are distractions, and they often mislead you.

"Simplicity is the key to brilliance." Bruce Lee

Yes, you have a million great ideas you are ready to implement, but just pick one and do it. Until you focus on just one thing, you will not finish.

Action Step: What can you do to simplify your goal? Just brainstorm. You can arrange your thoughts in the next lesson.

Baby Steps Are Required

It is easy to feel overwhelmed when you do something new, and this is completely normal. Take a deep breath and exhale. Are you still with me? Good. You can't do everything at once. You're not a robot, and it'll take time to reach your goal.

How can you sort through the confusion and move forward? Just take intentional baby steps.

> "When eating an elephant, take one bite at a time." Creighton Abrams

Instead of freaking out, turn your goal into bite-size tasks with definitive stopping points.

Achieve small daily victories. Don't worry about making the perfect order of tasks; you can always modify the order later. Just focus on the work at hand.

Success reinforces success.

Action Step: Break down your goal into tasks. What will you need to do? If you're not sure, start by writing down what you KNOW will have to happen. Don't worry about perfection, just write.

Examples

Goal: Go on family vacation to Disney World in July by sticking to a household budget.

Steps:
Figure out cost.
Save amount of money each month for trip.
Find available discounts.
Cut expenses.
Increase income.

Goal: Lose 20 lbs. by working out on my lunch hour three times a week over the next 90 days.

Steps:
Protect my lunch schedule.
Pack clothes for workout.
Figure out how many calories burned per workout.
Figure out how many calories I eat per day.

Goal:

Steps:

Make a Project To-do List

The last lesson mentioned the importance of intentional baby steps to achieve goals. Let's take this one step further and apply this concept to one of the biggest challenges—multistep projects. While a project with multiple steps is more involved than a one-time task, it doesn't have to be complicated.

Remember that all projects have a beginning, middle, and end.

Whether the project is building a bridge, writing a play, or starting a business, the project always has a beginning, middle, and end.

If you are stuck, start at the end and work your way backwards. Sort out your thoughts. Many of the things you want to focus on may be in the middle or end—so you don't have to worry about them right now.

Don't worry about the details yet—think about the big picture. You might view this as an outline, which is totally fine. It doesn't matter what you call it. Just focus on the entire process, and break it in stages or pieces.

Try to build a roadmap to completion, if you can. If you cannot put your thoughts in order yet, don't worry. The most important step is to get them down on paper.

Action Step: Turn one of your projects (maybe even your goal) into a project to-do list. This list will help you sort everything out and move forward. Again, remember all endeavors have a beginning, middle, and end.

Example

Writing an ebook

Idea/topic
Outline
Rough draft
Editing process
Marketing/launch
Up for sale

Your Project To-do List

Insert Stopping Points

Now that you have created a project to-do list, it's time to refine it more. You have to have limits in place, or you will not know where you are.

What is the smallest piece you can finish and feel good about?

Figure that out and you have the minimum daily requirement needed for your project to move forward.

It is much easier to do a specific task than it is to do an undefined longer project. When something lacks definition, it has the potential to grow before your eyes. When it grows suddenly, a project can spin out of control. Don't allow that— assign stopping points and you can make this a part of your daily routine.

Action Step: Create stopping points in your project to do list.

Example

Writing an ebook

Choose idea/figure out topic
Outline — stopping point

Write rough draft
Chapters 1–2 — stopping point

Chapters 3–4 — stopping point
Chapters 5–6 —stopping point
Chapters 7–8 — stopping point

Edit
Edit chapters 1–3 — stopping point
Edit chapters 4–6 — stopping point
Edit chapters 7–8 — stopping point

Get beta readers and graphic designer
Select and email beta readers — stopping point
Book cover and formatting — stopping point
Find and select designer — stopping point

Conduct marketing and launch
Inquire about, interviews, and reviews — stopping point
Confirm and do interviews, and reviews — stopping point

Put ebook up for sale Select service and schedule release date — stopping point

Insert Stopping Points in your Project To-do List

Refine Your Stopping Points

Figuring out your stopping points can be the messiest part of the process.

Some tasks will take longer than you expect, so give yourself space with time estimates.

The work you are doing must align with the time allotted, or you will set yourself up for headaches every time and also kill momentum, morale, and any progress. Don't let that happen! Change your time frames and move stopping points as needed. This is what was done below with the editing of the ebook. Instead of three chapters being edited at a time, it was revised to two chapters.

Some parts of projects do not have clean stopping points. It is your job to create them! For example, in the "select and email beta readers" task, I did not receive emails in the same time frame. The task did not have a clean break because I had received only 7 replies of the 10 emails sent.

Give yourself some flexibility to make your project list complete. You can always label it with more information as I did below. Julie, Mike, and Jon did not reply to my first email, so I revised my project list as needed.

Give yourself enough space to finish the work. If you don't, you will get burned out. Expect some interruptions and know you have to be proactive to stay on top.

Action Step: Take some time to think about your task list, and revise your stopping points.

Example

Writing an ebook

Choose idea/figure out topic

Outline — stopping point

Write rough draft

Chapters 1–2 — stopping point

Chapters 3–4 — stopping point

Chapters 5–6 —stopping point

Chapters 7–8 — stopping point

Edit

Edit chapters 1–2 — stopping point **<— originally three chapters**

Edit chapters 3–4 — stopping point **<— originally three chapters**

Edit chapters 5–6 — stopping point **<— originally three chapters**

Edit chapters 7–8 — stopping point **<— originally three chapters**

Get beta readers

Select and email beta readers — stopping point

Follow up with beta readers: Julie, Mike, and Jon — stopping point **<— details added**

Follow up again with beta readers: Mike — stopping point **<— details added**

Have book cover designed and book formatted **<— originally part of previous section**

Find and select graphic designer — stopping point

Conduct marketing and launch

Inquire about interviews, and reviews
Confirm and do interviews, and reviews — stopping point
Put ebook up for sale
Select service and schedule release date — stopping point

Go back to page 39 and revise your stopping points as needed. It is likely you won't be able to revise this until you are closer to achieving your goal.

Reflection: Process Your Progress

Legend has it that Benjamin Franklin set aside time to ask two questions every day. In the morning he asked himself: "What good shall I do today?" and in the evening he followed up with "What good have I done today?"

So on that note, take some time to think about how far you have come in the pursuit of your goal. It is easy to focus on today or the future and not look back. Don't make that mistake.

> *"Follow effective action with quiet reflection. From the quiet reflection will come even more effective action." Peter Drucker*

As you work toward your goal, it is essential to stop and gauge where you are. This step gives perspective and can help you make wise decisions as you move forward.

Action Step: Take some time to answer these questions:

Are you happy with your progress?

Is there any way you can avoid or minimize a weakness that is causing you trouble?

Does something have to change for you to meet your goal?

Face Your Fears

It can be scary to start new things. The voices in your head say things like "Who are you to do this?" or "Why do you think you can accomplish this goal? You're a failure."

Fear is made up of 99.99% lies. A lie with a hint of truth is still a lie. You can accomplish your goal, and it is completely up to you and no one else.

Don't have a conversation with your fears; talking with them will only make them grow as they attempt to rationalize with you. Instead, make a bold statement and get to work. Say: "Hi, fear! I'm going to keep hustling and pursuing my goal. If you want to stick around, that's fine—but I'm completely ignoring you." Fear hates hard work but loves procrastination. This truth manifests itself in thoughts like "Not today; I'll do it tomorrow."

Action Step: What fears are standing in your way? Write them down right now. Fear has more power when you keep it inside. When you write down your fear, the lies fall apart. Then debunk the fear to expose the lie. Now that you have confirmed that each idea is a lie, it's time to get to work.

Examples

Fear says "You're too old to pursue your goal."
Such a lie. If you are still breathing, you are not too old to pursue a goal.

Fear says "You're too young to do that."
Just another lie. One minute, fear says you are too old to do something, and another minute, fear says you are too young. Fear is the ultimate liar.

Fear says "You are a fraud."
We all struggle and fall short at times. Falling short doesn't mean you are a fraud; it means you are human. No one is perfect. The message that you are a fraud is just a lie to get you to stop from attempting a goal in the first place. When this kind of fear pops up, its occurrence often is a red flag you are doing something worthwhile.

What are your fears? Be brutally honest. Fear is the biggest roadblock to success.

Power Lies in Your Routine

Now that you know what you are going to work on, you need a routine. Routines are incredibly powerful because they set the tone for the day.

The difference between extraordinary and the status quo lies in your routine.

On the Beyond the To-Do List podcast, Erik asks almost every guest the question "In an ideal world, how do you start your day?" Cliff Ravenscraft responded, "You're not going to fall into a good, healthy, wonderful productive routine just by chance. It has to be something you have purposefully done."

Select a time to work on your goal, and stick to it. Don't rely on your memory. Just write down what you are going to do— choosing a work time will keep things as simple as possible.

> "The secret of your future is hidden in your daily routine." Mike Murdock

Small smart choices over time bring radical results.

Action Step: What would be the ideal way to start your day? What steps can you take to do this each day?

Don't take your routine lightly. What you do first sets the tone for the entire day.

Example

Get up.
Drink coffee.
Eat breakfast.
Read for 15 minutes.
Write for 35 minutes.
Work out for 40 minutes.
Shower.

What would be the ideal way to start your day?

What does your current routine look like?

What steps can you take to improve your current routine?

Know Your Strengths

It's hard to be a good gauge of yourself. Your strengths often come naturally to you, so they are hard to notice.
How do you resolve this? Take a strengths test.

> *"Know thyself." Socrates*

There are several strengths tests you can take, some include a book or there are even some free online. (See the references section on page 94 for a link to a free test.) It's important to know what your strengths are as you plan out your goal. Emphasize your strengths, and use them to find success.

> *"Hide not your talents. They for use were made. What's a sundial in the shade?" Benjamin Franklin*

Action Step: Take a strengths test to determine your strengths.

Example
Strengths Test Results
1. Empathy
2. Belief
3. Developer
4. Inclusiveness
5. Input

Whatever your strengths are, it is possible you are not using them intentionally right now. Now is the time to change that! It's also a good idea to retake the strengths test in 60 to 90 days just to see how much the results vary. If you are extremely stressed when you take it—or sleep deprived—that could easily change your responses.

What are your results from the strengths test? Next to each strength, write down your initial thoughts of where you think this is being applied in your life. If it is not currently, when did you last use it?

Know Your Weaknesses

After spending some time focusing on your strengths, it's time to take a look at your weaknesses. When you are aware of your weaknesses, you also know when to ask for assistance (and in what areas)—this is a very valuable lesson!

Have a really messy desk? You probably struggle with being disorganized and face challenges making decisions. This reality can permeate your entire life.

To work on this, you can ask for help from others and decide how to simplify your life.

Messiness can become a strength when you use it as an opportunity to delegate the work of organizing to others or when you do the work anyway and build up your level of self-discipline.

Are you blunt when you interact with others? This habit leads to communication issues, and others might view you as rude. To alleviate this, you could add "please" or "thanks so much" or even "sent on the run; please excuse the brevity" as part of your email signature on the phone, and that simple addition could completely change how others feel when they interact with you.

Being blunt is not just a weakness—it is also a strength. Being blunt means you are direct and clear in communication.

"Out of your vulnerabilities will come your strength." Sigmund Freud

Action Step: Ask yourself: What are four of my weaknesses? Reflect and jot down your thoughts. If you're not sure, think about some of the areas you struggle with the most. You can also ask five close friends for their input. It is scary to ask, but once you find out your weaknesses, you will grow and mature.

Example
Indecisiveness
Blunt
Messy
Easily angered

What are four of your weaknesses?

Discipline Is Needed

Discipline is rare in an "instantly satisfied" culture. Think about it: how often do you cook popcorn on the stove instead of the microwave or write a letter by hand instead of an email?

The easy way is almost always more attractive than the hard way.

But if you want success, the easy way is likely the path to be avoided. Embrace discipline and put in the work. Discipline is not your enemy; it is one of your greatest allies.

Pain will happen. It is inevitable. Your response is what you control.

> "We must all suffer one of two things: the pain of discipline or the pain of regret or disappointment." Jim Rohn

You can do it. Do something the "hard way" today. Wake up early. Stay up late. And when you do this, notice that the voices in your head shift from "I can't" to "I know I can."

Action Step: Write out what you are doing and why you are doing it. Many times fear is a part of discipline. When you write out why you are doing something, fear often dissipates.

Examples

I am working on a business plan instead of sleeping, because I will be filled with regret if I don't share my product with the world.

I am learning how to code because I want to design applications that no one else is making.

What are you doing and why are you doing it?

Get Motivated Visually

When you see something in your mind, a part of you believes it as true.

> *"If you can see it, and believe it, it is much easier to achieve it." Oprah Winfrey*

Your subconscious pulls you in a direction. If you already believe you are a success, do you think that belief will lead to a more positive life or a more negative life?

Jim Carrey was once a struggling unknown comedian in Los Angeles. At night, he would drive up to the Hollywood sign and stay there until he felt successful. Once Jim felt confident, then he would drive home feeling great about himself, knowing it was just a matter of when he would be successful, not if.

> *"I wrote myself a check for 10 million dollars for acting services rendered and dated it Thanksgiving 1995. I put it in my wallet, and it deteriorated. And then, just before Thanksgiving, I found out I was going to make 10 million dollars for Dumb & Dumber." Jim Carrey*

Studies have revealed mental workouts are almost as effective as physical workouts. In one example, mental training led to a 35% increase in finger strength and a 13.5% in elbow flexion strength.[3]

Why not use this tool to your advantage? Visualize your success and accomplish more today.

Action Step: Find something that can motivate you visually and use it to your advantage.

Examples

If you want to be a musician, attend a concert by one of your favorite musical artists.

If you are a writer, go to a bookstore or library. Take a picture of the bookshelf you want to have your book go on.

If your goal is to go to a certain college, get your picture taken by the entrance.

What is a way you can motivate yourself visually?

Reflection: Give Yourself Grace

Your mind will wander as you pursue your goal. You cannot become disciplined overnight—it will take time. Do what you can.

> *"Some beats none. Some business planning always beats none. Some dreaming always beats none. Some whatever it is you're passionate about, always beats none."* Jon Acuff

As you learn and grow, you will fall down. Don't beat yourself up. Think positive thoughts. Know that you can and will do this. Don't let fear tell you this is all or nothing.

> *"Act as if what you do makes a difference. It does."* William James

Action Step: Revisit the reasons why you are pursuing your goal on page 28. Let these reasons help you refocus and motivate yourself at the same time. Revise if needed.

Don't Fall into the Comparison Trap

As you keep working on your goal, you will want to compare yourself with others and contrast them against you. Try your best not to fall into this mindset since it often leads to negativity. When you struggle, you will notice others who excel. Focusing on their successes and contrasting those against your own (or your lack of success) can cause resentment. You are likely contrasting your beginning against someone's middle or end. With regular exposure to social media such as Facebook or Twitter, you might even find yourself contrasting your blooper reel against another's highlight reel.

To avoid this trap altogether, be quick to give a compliment. Instead of being negative and tearing others down, think: "Wow, this is a great opportunity to learn.

A positive attitude is a gift you can use to propel yourself and others forward and to enjoy life to the fullest.

Action Step: Compliment someone today as the person pursues a goal, regardless of how you are doing with your own.

Example
If your goal is to lose weight and you find out that a friend has just lost some weight, instead of being jealous, congratulate your friend, and ask for pointers.

Name of person (or several people if you'd like) to compliment and how you will do it.

Lay One Brick at a Time

Here's a secret you already know: achieving a goal is often really hard. With any type of growth comes pain. As you push forward and continue to grind through challenges, know you are much closer to the end than you realize.

> *"Don't try to build a wall. You don't say I'm going to build the greatest wall that's ever been built. You don't start there. You take a brick and you say, 'I'm going to lay this brick as perfectly as a brick can be laid.' And then you do it every day. And soon you have a wall." Will Smith*

Keep laying bricks. Momentum is very powerful.

Action Step: Step back and look at the progress you've made. Let this encourage you to work on another brick today.

What do you think when you look back at what you've done so far?

Are you satisfied with what you've accomplished? Why or why not?

How You Think Is Everything

Do you think positively or negatively? How you think drives your success.

> "Attitude is a little thing that makes a very big difference." Winston Churchill

Your past does not define you. Let me repeat that for those who are so filled with fear but don't even realize it—your past does not define you. Fear of failure or even fear of repeating failure can dominate your life. Don't let it!

You can choose to focus on the negatives or on the positives. It's completely up to you.

> "Whether you think you can or you can't, you're right." Henry Ford

Start your day out with a good attitude, and you can completely change your life. You decide how things will go. You and you alone must want to achieve your goal. Surround yourself with encouraging, upbeat friends. Iron sharpens iron—so surround yourself with others who strengthen and hone you.

Action Step: Write down 10 things you have done that made you feel good about yourself.

Example

1. Placing in the top 10 in an art contest

2. Riding dirt bikes on trails

3. Making the game-winning shot

4. Encouraging a friend in need

5. Losing some extra weight

6. Getting a hug from my daughter

7. Hearing a baby laugh

8. Learning a song on the guitar

9. Finishing an exam

10. Being complimented by someone I respect

What 10 things have you done that made you feel good about yourself? Use the space below.

1.

2.

3.

4.

5.

6.

7.

8.

9.

10.

Support Is Needed

Pursuing big goals is a roller coaster with high highs and low lows, so you will need support. Remember—even the Lone Ranger had Tonto. And Silver too.

> *"Support from others is critical to your success. When you have support, the voices of encouragement soften the negative voices in your head." Tammy Helfrich*

You will need support from people on several levels.

The first level is to have the support of your spouse. Your spouse needs to be your biggest cheerleader and to realize how badly you want to achieve your goal. You need to talk with your husband or wife the most and let him or her know what is really going on. If your spouse isn't on board yet, that's fine—put in the hustle to communicate that you are serious. Talk is not what changes your life; action is.

If you are single, have your first level of support come from a close friend or a parent. You too need support!

Secondly, you need support from at least three others who are in the trenches with you and have first-hand experience in the same area. For example, if you are a writer, get support from other writers or artists.

If you are married, be very, very careful about how you approach this—social sites such as Facebook are one of the top sources for evidence in divorce proceedings.[4] Talk with your spouse and set agreed-upon boundaries in this area to avoid these kind of issues. Don't put yourself in any questionable situations; it's better to err on the side of caution.

Thirdly, it's a good idea to have a "brag table" as well. What is a brag table? It is a place to share your wins with others. Wins need to be celebrated. Some also call this a mastermind group. You can find out more about this kind of group in the resources section of the book.

You may want to pursue goals alone, but to succeed you need the support of your family and friends. They want you to succeed. Talk with them and spend quality time with them. They are not holding you back—they are the ones lifting you up.

Action Step: Start compiling a list of names of people you want in your first, second, and third levels of support. The first level is the most important level. If you don't have anyone there, please start there first and then move to the other levels.

Example:

First Level: Your husband or wife takes the kids out of the house for a few hours each week to give you time to work on your goal.

Second Level: Have one friend text you every other day (or more if needed) and another call you once a week just to give you support, encouragement, and accountability.

Third Level: Get together with a writers group once a month in person, or have a Google Hangout with several friends online.

What do your levels of support consist of? If you don't have them in place, what would you like them to consist of? Who can you connect with today?

1.

2.

3.

When You Want to Quit

At some point, you'll want to give up.

But don't quit. You have grown so much already, and you will grow even more when you face adversity.

> *"If you're going through hell, keep going."*
> *Winston Churchill*

Henry Ford failed with two companies before he finally succeeded.

The movie *Star Wars: A New Hope* was rejected by every movie studio in Hollywood before 20th Century Fox produced it. Then the movie went on to be one of the largest grossing movies in film history.[5]

Steve Jobs was fired from the company he co-founded at the age of 30. In his own words, "the heaviness of being successful was replaced by the lightness of being a beginner again, less sure about everything. It freed me to enter one of the most creative periods of my life."[6] And it was during this period Steve created Pixar, the most successful animation studio in the world.

He then went on to create the iPhone®, iPad®, and countless other devices. Dr. Seuss's first children's book, *And to Think That I Saw it on Mulberry Street*, was rejected by 27 publishers. The 28th publisher, Vanguard Press, sold six million copies of the book.

Anything worth doing requires pain and discomfort. Keep going and don't quit!

> "Don't limit yourself. Many people limit themselves to what they think they can do. You can go as far as your mind lets you." Mary Kay Ash

Action Step: Call a member of your inner circle for support. Get some encouragement—you need it right now. Never underestimate the power that hope brings. Watch an uplifting movie, listen to some positive music, or go for a walk. Now is not the time to sit around feeling sorry for yourself.

What did your friend say to encourage you?

What are your takeaways from the conversation?

Reflection: Don't Overdo It

We all know how the race with the tortoise and the hare ended. The tortoise, the slower competitor, won!

Pace yourself. You won't accomplish your goal on the first day or first week.

The veteran is in this for the long haul, while the rookie focuses on only today.

> "Don't underestimate yourself. You are capable and will achieve great things. It will be slow, but slow and steady wins the race every time." Ben Dempsey

Work on small steps over time, and focus on your task list. You will build momentum and feel progress.

> "We often feel like we need to change 33 things yesterday, but that's not realistic. Instead, pick one small thing to change. It might not seem like much, but if you commit to change 1 thing every three months, that's 4 changes in a year. Over 10 years, that's 40 changes in your life. It may feel like you are barely making any change, but over time it's going to add up to very significant change." Crystal Paine

Action Step: Take a few moments to think about how far you've come. Spend five minutes reflecting on your progress and write down your thoughts. Let this evidence encourage you and motivate you as you go forward.

What are some of your thoughts as you reflect back on your journey toward your goal? Spend only a few minutes on this and take a break. You've earned it!

Move Past the Rats

Have you ever seen the movie *First Blood* (Rambo)? One of the most powerful scenes is one in which Rambo is alone and injured in a dark, cold cave. After reaching several dead ends, eventually Rambo finds himself in a tight space being attacked by rats. He frantically moves forward instead of retreating back. He pushes further. And then even further. Finally, he finds a way out.

The same thing often happens with goals. Do you stop or do you move forward when the rats—the haters, illness, sleepless nights—attack? What if the challenges are just another dead-end ahead? It doesn't matter. Keep pushing forward, even if your progress is only one inch at a time.

You have to want your goal more than anyone else. While support is important, your success ultimately depends on you.

> *"Sometimes life hits you in the head with a brick.*
> *Don't lose faith. "* Steve Jobs

Action Step: Don't stop—you are so close to the end now.

What last steps do you need to take? Plan out what you can in small steps.

Perfectionism Kills Dreams

Nothing is ever perfect.

You are doing something new. You won't do it perfectly right now. You are learning and growing. It's impossible to be an expert at something new.

Keep this in mind as you move forward. Even when you stumble and fall, know that stumbling and falling are inevitable. Nothing is perfect. Keep working. Keep pushing. Don't give up.

> *"Too many people spend too much time trying to perfect something before they actually do it. Instead of waiting for perfection, run with what you got, and fix it along the way."* Paul Arden

Push as hard as you can. But when the deadline comes, finish, and then it's time for the next project.

"Real artists ship." Steve Jobs

Action Step: We all have some perfectionist tendencies; don't embrace them. Instead, refer to your action plan and make a decision. Indecisiveness goes hand-in-hand with perfectionism. Do whatever you have to do to finish and achieve your goal.

What final decisions do you have to make?

It's Time to Finish

Your goal is in sight. You're almost there. Keep moving forward. Don't stop. Keep pushing. Continue to make the decisions you need to make. Don't quit now—keep going!

Fear will attack you right before you accomplish your goal. It always happens. Expect it, and you won't be taken by surprise.

Many 99% finished books have spent their lives in closets, cabinets, and drawers due to fear.

"Never, never, never give up." Winston Churchill

Don't give in. Make this last dash and cross the finish line.

Action Step: It's time to finish. Do whatever it takes. Keep moving forward and don't stop.

When You Fail

After all of this hard work, you failed. Sorry! Failure is inevitable. No matter what you do, if you put yourself out there, sometimes what you do will not resonate with others. You may not hit your goal weight despite eating healthier and working out. Your novel might not be ready to be published. The question now is, what will you do about it?

Do you give up? No way!

Failure can also be a state of mind—you feel as if you yourself are a failure. But you're not!

Experiencing various failures in your lifetime does not mean you are a failure as a human being. If you have a positive attitude, it will minimize the sting. Sure it hurts, but to be successful, you must not quit when you fail.

It's normal to be sad, frustrated, mad, and even depressed at this time. Go ahead—give yourself some grace, and take a couple days off to reflect on the journey you've been on. But know that success is found when you stick with it.

Don't be too hard on yourself. Celebrate any accomplishments you have achieved. If you lost 10 pounds and your goal was 20 pounds, don't sweat it! You still lost 10 pounds!

If your goal was to write an ebook and all you have is a rough draft—you still have a rough draft! Build on what you've accomplished. You will continue to improve over time.

<u>Don't ever, ever, ever give up!</u>

When You Succeed

Congratulations—you succeeded! Well done! Take some time to celebrate. Let your friends and family also know you succeeded. If possible, join them, and have a party together or go to your favorite restaurant.

What are some other things you can do?

Here are some ideas:

1. Take a mini vacation for the weekend.
2. Support and encourage others as they pursue their goals.
3. Treat yourself with a gift such as a Fitbit, new shoes, and so forth that you can use for other goals.
4. Do something you enjoy but rarely have time to do such as going camping.
5. Go out on a date with your spouse or friends.
6. Two words: bacon party.
7. Go out to the movies.
8. Catch up on one of your favorite TV shows.
9. Go to Chuck E. Cheese®.
10. Spend the day outside doing your favorite activities.

Take Time to Review

After the deadline has passed for your goal, whether you've succeeded or failed, the time has come to ask some important questions and reflect on the entire process.

Did you accomplish your goal? Why or why not?

What advice would you give to someone pursuing the same goal?

What would you like to improve from this process?

What do you want to remember for the future?

Now go back to the beginning, and get started on your next goal!

Page intentionally left blank for your notes

Resources

Test Yourself

Personality tests are a great way to learn about yourself. Each of the following links takes you to a free online test.

Strengthsfinder test — This test takes inventory of your strengths.

Myers-Briggs-based test — This test gives you a four-letter formula such as INFP or ENFJ, based on four areas and tells you celebrities who have the same personality profile.

DISC-based test — This test helps you determine your DISC type: **D**ominance, **I**nfluence, **S**teadiness, and **C**ompliance.

You can access all of these tests by visiting www.readyaimfirebook.com/resources

Note: these free online tests are not as in depth or accurate as the longer tests available for sale.

Action Step: If you want to get the most out of these tests, take one every other day for a week, and write down your results. Then take the tests again a month later to compare–contrast and see if you get the same results.

Get a Lift

There is a free application called Lift that you can use to help you achieve your goals. It is available in an online web version and an iPhone mobile version.
(Just go to **www.readyaimfirebook.com/resources** for the links to this application.)

From reading each day to drinking more water, the app offers different habits and tasks for you to choose from. Then you mark them off as you do them. As you complete the habits, over time you build momentum. You can also encourage others and receive encouragement.

You can use Lift as a daily task list and add new goals to your routine over time. Don't be afraid of the "easy wins" such as saying "I love you" to your spouse and brushing your teeth. Once you check off a few tasks, you'll find it easier to complete the entire list.

Action Step: Give Lift a try, and see if it works for you. You can also check out episode #59 of Beyond The To Do List which interviews Tony Stubblebine, the Co-Founder of the application.

Free Online Resources

You can access all of these resources by visiting www.readyaimfirebook.com/resources

Video Summary of How to Pursue Goals

Simon Sinek "Start with Why" video

Chris Locurto's "Zig Ziglar's Wheel of Life"

Pat Flynn's Podcast Episode Focusing on Productivity

Michael Hyatt's Ideal Day

Michael Hyatt's "The Beginner's Guide to Goal Setting"

Online stopwatch

"Thinking About Starting a Business? 10 Steps to Starting a Business"

"Business Planning Guide" by Dan Miller

"6 Steps to Finding a Teacher, Mentor or Coach"

Highly Recommended Resources

You can access direct links to purchase these resources by visiting www.readyaimfirebook.com/resources

Say Goodbye to Survival Mode: 9 Simple Strategies to Stress Less, Sleep More, and Restore Your Passion for Life by Crystal Paine

Start: Punch Fear in the Face, Escape Average and Do Work that Matters by Jon Acuff

Switch: How to Change Things When Change Is Hard by Dan and Chip Heath

Decisive: How to Make Better Choices in Life and Work by Dan and Chip Heath

Failing Forward: Turning Mistakes into Stepping Stones for Success by John C. Maxwell

Do the Work by Steven Pressfield

The War of Art: Break Through the Blocks and Win Your Inner Creative Battles by Steven Pressfield

A Gift for You

As a special bonus for buying this book, you are invited to download the audio version narrated by Erik Fisher.

Just go to www.readyaimfirebook.com/audiobook and pick up your copy today.

Acknowledgements

Erik would like to thank ...

First and foremost, I want to thank God for life and creativity.

I want to thank my awesome wife, Beth, who has patience with me (one of the best productivity tools). My creative daughter, Emily, who wears me out but in a good way. My son, Evan, who always makes me laugh with his energy.

Jim Woods, for having the vision that this collaboration would work. Jon Acuff, for inspiration and instruction, without which we wouldn't have 'START'ed this. Cliff Ravenscraft for being a great friend and showing what consistent podcasting looks like.

Jim would like to thank ...

God, the ultimate Creator.

My amazing family: Kristal, Kate, and Jack. I love you all so much!

Erik Fisher, the ambassador of bacon; Jesse Hoover, the donut king; Tammy Helfrich, the ultimate encourager; Chris Morris, the hope-giver; Ben Dempsey, the ultimate health coach; Jared Easley, the ultimate challenger; Sarah Mae, the ebook expert; Jon Acuff, the fear-puncher; and Elizabeth Hyndman and Andrea Hultman, the ultimate editing team.

To all the readers—thank you! This book would not be possible without you.

Notes

[1] Smart Criteria http://en.wikipedia.org/wiki/SMART_criteria

[2] Goals Study by Dominican University
http://cdn.sidsavara.com/wp-
content/uploads/2008/09/researchsummary2.pdf

[3] Mental study
http://www.ncbi.nlm.nih.gov/pubmed/14998709

[4] Facebook proceedings top issue in divorce.
http://www.theguardian.com/technology/2011/mar/08/faceb
ook-us-divorces

[5] Star Wars Rejected by All Major studios
http://www.huffingtonpost.com/2008/05/16/george-lucas-
on-indiana-j_n_102077.html

[6] Steve Jobs Fired
http://news.stanford.edu/news/2005/june15/jobs-
061505.html

Quotes from Crystal Paine, Michael Hyatt, Ben Dempsey, Jon Acuff, Bryan Allain, and Cliff Ravenscraft were given direct permission. All other quotes are considered public domain.

Page intentionally left blank for your notes

Page intentionally left blank for your notes

Page intentionally left blank for your notes

Page intentionally left blank for your notes